"The WHACK Life"

Written by: Todd Anthony Hutchinson

First Edition

Copyright © 2025, All Rights Reserved

Published by TKS Venture Holdings, LLC

McKinney, TX

tksvhllc@gmail.com

ISBN #979-8-9995244-0-9 (Paperback)

ISBN #979-8-9995244-1-6 (e-book)

Book Cover Design:

Contents

Chapter 1 What are Goals?

A famous Harvard study from the 1970s has become the foundation for most modern goal-setting ideas. The study revealed that, among a class of MBA program students, only three percent had written down their goals and plans. Thirteen percent had goals but had not written them down. The other 84 percent of the graduates had no goals at all, just a diploma in their hands. Ten years later, an amazing result was revealed. The three percent of graduates who had written down their goals and plans had amassed a net worth ten times higher than the other 97 percent of their peers! The 13 percent who had goals in mind at least had twice as much net worth as the 84 percent of graduates with no goals.

This famous study clearly demonstrates that having goals and plans, and writing them down, is the first step to achieving success and surpassing others.

When it comes to finances, this study proves that writing your goals down is crucial to help you achieve the wealth that you desire. We all know life is *not* just about wealth. This book will illuminate that point. If properly utilized, the practice of writing goals will subsequently benefit other areas in your life. These include the spiritual, physical, and relational areas of your life, in addition to your dreams, desires, and bucket list items. In this book, you will:

- **WRITE** down your goals
- build healthy **HABITS**
- **ACHIEVE** your goals
- **CELEBRATE** your accomplishments
- **KEEP** repeating the process

Now you know why the book is titled *The WHACK Life!*

I've done amazing things in my life, from singing onstage to recording music, being a part of films and television shows, writing screenplays, stage plays, songs, and novels, to ministering and pastoring all over the United States. I have a beautiful and wonderful wife of over 26 years. A talented and intelligent son, of whom I am extremely proud. I have a loving and supportive family and friends. Most of everything I have achieved in life has come about through two important factors. First and foremost, it is by the grace of God. Two, from an early age, I understood the practice of dreaming about something and then writing down a road map to achieve it. I want to share the simple tools I have used for over 40 years, in the hope that if there are some unfulfilled desires in your life, maybe this will help you begin the process of achieving them. Let us begin with the first question: What is a goal?

Merriam-Webster has three main definitions of the word 'goal.' Two of those three definitions involve sports-related topics. An area or object toward which players in various games attempt to advance a ball, puck, or object, usually through or into which it must go to score points. The act or action of causing a ball, puck, or object through or into such a goal. The score resulting from such an act. The terminal point of a race. An area to be reached safely in children's games. This makes sense since we know that in major sports here in America, you shoot a basket through the ten-foot hanging net to score a goal, in hockey you shoot a puck into the net to score a goal, and in football you kick a pigskin through the uprights to score a field goal. The definition we will focus most on in this book is this one: the end toward which effort is directed.

The end result! Having something to be accomplished and pursued. Some synonyms that paint a bigger picture are aim, ambition, aspiration, dream, idea, ideal, intent, intention, meaning, objective, plan, purpose, target, and many more. You get the picture. A goal is a destination and the pursuit of something. If I'm traveling from Texas to Florida, my goal is Florida. How I achieve that goal is the plan. There is no plan without a goal. Do I take 1-10 all the way, then 95 down? Should I take a more scenic route? It will take longer, but maybe I want to visit some tiny towns along the way. My goal is clear; my plan depends on how I want to reach that goal.

What types of goals are there? There are thousands of goals; a goal can be applied to almost every aspect of life. In this book, we will focus mainly on two areas of your life and the goals we set in them. Professional and Personal goals are what we will focus on. We will also focus on time-sensitive goals. Short-term and long-term. Short-term goals can be daily, weekly, monthly, quarterly, and yearly goals you set to achieve. Long-term goals will consist of goals you have that may take several years or even a decade to achieve. Almost all of your long-term goals will consist of achieving your short-term goals.

Why are goals important? The Harvard study underscored the results aspect of goals. Goals also provide important things like structure. A goal provides a destination; to achieve that destination, you need a plan. A plan provides a detailed structure on how to achieve that goal. The more goals you have, the more plans you have, and the more structure you can establish around your life. Goals also provide guidance. Maybe you have a weight loss goal (as do most people). Making adjustments to your eating habits and exercise gives you proper direction to sustain a healthier lifestyle. Goals also create landmarks in your life. Maybe you want to own your own home one day. If so, you set yourself a landmark. Maybe you say by the time I'm twenty-five or thirty; I want to own a home. This landmark gives you a purpose and a plan to financially prepare yourself for that achievement. Maybe you set some stronger discipline around what you earn and spend. This landmark and the goal to reach it may create in you a more fiscally responsible person. Maybe it is retirement. A landmark is a future and major destination.

Goals are also like a horizon. A fixed point in the distance to which you direct your compass. Goals are navigation tools. Like sailors in the night, the stars are their goals. They know if they lock onto a fixed celestial object in the sky, they will be moving in the right direction. Goals, most importantly, are designed to help you grow. The more goals you set and either achieve or fail, the more you learn what you are capable of. The more you learn what you need to improve on, the more inevitably you grow. Maybe this is something you have never done before in your life, and someone or something has compelled you to try it.

The last and most important action to do with goals is to write them down. Some use journals, others day planners, and some put goals on a napkin when they think about them. However it works for you, the secret is writing them down, making a record of what they are. As you go through this book, I hope you take notes or highlight the items that you are inspired to pursue. According to the Harvard study, a majority of people reading this book have never made goals or written them down. Hopefully, this book will inspire you to become a regular goal setter and to see your life change in a positive way. Let's begin!

Chapter 2 Write Down Your Goals!

The first step to achieving any goal is simple: write it down! We do this in other areas all the time. Maybe some of you wing it at the grocery store, but I found when I do that, I spend more money than I wanted to.

My goal at the grocery store is to get the things that I am lacking in my pantry, freezer, and refrigerator. I usually look inside those three areas and write down on paper the items I need. That is my goal, to acquire those items. Do I end up grabbing a few more items, of course? When I forget the list, and my goal isn't in front of me, I typically forget a crucial item like butter, bread, coffee, or toilet paper that would have been written down on my list. Simple illustration, but very relatable.

When you write something down there is a greater chance you will not forget it. Where you keep your goals is important too. When items are needed around the house, I found the refrigerator is the best place since not a day goes by that you do not open the fridge. Your bathroom mirror is the second place to keep your goals and things to do. You are in your bathroom every day as well. There are two items I keep in my briefcase, on my desk and at my home office all the time: my weekly/monthly day planner and my everyday journal.

At the beginning of each year, I put my yearly goals down in my journal and day planner. At the beginning of each month, I put down goals I want to achieve in those months. Writing down and having to look at it every day keeps the goals fresh in my mind. I know what you are thinking: Why don't you just put it in your handy-dandy cell phone or tablet? Two reasons! One, I'm old school. Two, just recently the Neurological department at the University of Tokyo did a study (Umejima et al., 2021) led by a team of researchers. The study was performed on 48 students and recent graduates. It was referred to as the "paper notebooks vs. mobile devices" study. They used fMRI neuroimaging to identify specific brain activation differences during memory retrieval.

The study concluded four specific advantages to writing things down on paper using a writing device versus typing it into an app on a mobile device. The first was time. Jotting things down on paper was faster than putting it into an app on phone or tablet. The study also concluded that handwritten notes tended to be more accurate and included personalized flairs which helped memory. While monitoring the students' brain activity the study concludes there was more brain activity utilized and triggered from writing something down instead of typing it into a device. Finally writing something by hand was associated with stronger neural encoding and memory retrieval.

The truth is there are less distractions when you write something down. Anytime you go to your phone or tablet to input something there are an unlimited amount of distractions available from Instagram to emails, to texts, to YouTube videos and memes. I know the younger generation have more skills when it comes to electronic devices, however, both the Harvard study and the University of Tokyo study both provide evidence of success when goals are physically written down.

I go one step further in my goal setting. When I write goals down, I write them down in pencil. Yes, a number 2 pencil to be exact. Why do you ask? Life happens. If I need to adjust something or move a timeline, it is easy to correct. Writing your goals down allows you to timestamp the event. If I put in my day planner in January of that year that I want to finish writing three non-fiction books this year, I have timestamped it. I know when I set the goal down and how long I gave myself to achieve that goal.

I do this with all goals. Maybe I want to read the bible in its entirety this year. I timestamp when I start that goal and have a 365-day deadline to finish. What if I gained ten pounds over the holiday season (it happens!) I notate in January that I want to lose those ten pounds by May, a solid goal of two pounds a month. I uncomfortably put my weight down on January 1st and on the first of the following months to track my goal.

Writing down your goals allows you to have a starting point, a measurable time, and an end date of achievement. Like creating a game plan. You write the goal down. You write down how you plan on accomplishing that goal. You write down when you wish that goal to be accomplished. Writing a goal, tracking a goal, and achieving a goal are equally important.

I will quietly admit that I love football, and my favorite team is the Miami Dolphins. I was born in Florida, so give me a break! Every year when the schedule comes out, I look at it and try to determine if the Dolphins can make it to the playoffs. Now I know in today's competitive landscape and with a 17-game schedule, you need a minimum of 10 or 11 wins to make the playoffs. If I were the head coach, my goal would be simple. Win your division games and win all your home games. That alone would garner 10 wins minimum. Your losses should only come to non-conference teams and teams that will not compete for the playoffs.

Regardless of what you are trying to achieve, weight loss, savings, a Caribbean vacation, a home purchase, to quit drinking, start a new business, anything you set your mind and heart to. Writing the goals, dreams, and visions down is the first step. There is a great scripture in the Bible from Habakkuk 2:2 that states, "Write the vision down plainly on tablets, so he may run who reads it." The Lord is speaking this to the Prophet Habakkuk. I love this because when you make your goals plain and write them down, anyone can come along, read them, and be able to run alongside you to help you accomplish them.

Whether you assess your goals every year like me or if you have never written down your goals, there is no time like the present! I have been a writer since I was thirteen. My brain never shuts off, and ideas flow in and out like the tide. So many good ideas have come lying in bed at night or while I'm driving. I don't write them all down and have lost them on a number of occasions. Especially if I'm up at two in the morning and a great idea came, I couldn't psych myself into getting up and writing it down. I repeated the idea in my mind over and over again, hoping it would stick. Come morning time, I couldn't remember.

The two studies mentioned should give you enough evidence that writing your goals down leads to success. Maybe your first goal should be to go out and buy a day planner, journal, pens, and pencils. That would be an easy goal to start with and one that will help you write down more goals. The homework I am going to give you for this chapter will be a basic exercise to begin with. Write down five areas of your life: spiritual, financial, physical, relational, and emotional. Once you have those written down, write three specific goals for each of those areas. After you have written those down, attach time-specific dates to achieve each goal. This is the best place to begin.

I'll give you an example of one of mine from this year. My physical goals this year were simple: get my weight under 200 pounds. I have been hovering between 201 and 208, way too heavy for my frame. My second goal was to intermittently fast every day from 9 pm till noon the next day and do three twenty-four-hour fasts a month. Basically, skip breakfast every day. My third physical goal was to drastically reduce sugar from my diet. I started in January. At the end of March, I weighed in at 198lbs. The fasting and cutting down on sugar were key to the weight loss, and specifically why I chose those goals. I feel better, my body looks better, and my clothes fit better. Writing the goal down and being specific helped me achieve my goal ahead of schedule.

In whatever area you want to accomplish something, practicing this method of writing down goals and making them time sensitive will help you tremendously in achieving them. Will you achieve all of them? No! The secret is to continually grow, write new goals down, keep track of what worked and didn't work, and adjust when necessary. Now that we have discussed the importance of writing down your goals, we will move into the most important aspect of achieving those goals, which is developing good and prosperous habits.

Consistency leads to success. Let's continue to grow!

Chapter 3 Habits Determine Your Progress

We all have habits. Some good, some bad. Before we get into how habits determine your goals, we will revisit an old friend, Merriam-Webster. Merriam-Webster describes the word *Habit* in three specific definitions. The first is a settled tendency or usual manner of behavior. The second is an acquired mode of behavior that has become nearly or completely involuntary. The third definition is a behavior pattern acquired by frequent repetition or physiologic exposure that shows itself in regularity or increased facility of performance. Those are some fancy words, so let me break it down for you in layman's terms or in my southern Florida cracker way. Habits are things you do repetitively, like the sun and the moon rising and setting. Habits are things that become second nature until you don't even realize you are doing them. Habits are formed by doing some stuff over and over again, or seeing someone else do them, and you don't want to be left out. Like I said above, we all have habits; some are good, some are bad.

The best way to achieve your goals is to create good habits around them. As I mentioned in the last chapter, one of my goals this year was to get my weight below 200 pounds. My height is around 5'11" and on a good day with my boots, I'll say 6'0". My frame is normally thin. After I got married, became a father, and had to get into corporate America, I gained a ton of weight due to stress and other factors. My weight shot above 200lbs., at the top I was 212. Very uncomfortable for my frame and my clothes. The goal I had written down was to get below the 200 threshold. One of the ways I planned on doing this was to create a good habit of intermittent fasting.

I read several studies and watched a number of videos on natural weight loss. The majority of the studies and videos had two major points in common that caused weight loss. Intermittent fasting and the mass reduction of sugar from your diet. Now I will admit, I wasn't a big breakfast eater. Most of the time, the only reason I ate breakfast was because of stress, and that stress usually led to a bad choice for breakfast, like donuts, kolaches, egg McMuffins, and other assorted fast-food items. The sugar intake, however, was a problem. I will admit that candy was my one true addiction. This started from an early age and would continue for most of my current life. Items like Skittles, Jelly Bellies, Red Twizzlers, Sour Patch Candies, Jordan Almonds, Dark Chocolate Bars, and Hostess Cake items. This sugar cornucopia all resided in what we called in our household "The Bucket." The bucket was normally full, especially around all the holidays.

This would be the hardest for me to curtail. I was determined to create some good habits to help reach my weight loss goal. The easiest habit I started right away was intermittent fasting. I would begin to have my last bit of food around 8 pm. I would not eat again until lunchtime, which was usually between noon and 1 pm the next day. So, for at least five out of the seven days a week, I was fasting for a good 16-17 hours a day. On busy days when work wouldn't allow me to eat lunch, I would go around 21-22 hours without eating. This one good habit made a huge difference. I saw my weight drop immediately with this habit. When I began to drastically cut down on all the candy and snacks that were in 'The Bucket," this good habit added to my weight loss, and within four months, I had met my weight loss goal. This weight loss also occurred with little exercise. Weight loss is more about diet and caloric intake than cardio and pushing dumbbells.

My goal could have easily been thwarted by a bad habit as well. I could have said, since I'm fasting most of the day, I need to have much bigger portions at night, or that it didn't matter what I ate. I would not have been successful if I stopped at Raising Cane's Chicken every night or ordered a pizza to be delivered while eating the whole pizza. I have seen many goals being unattained because someone neutralized a good habit by adding a bad habit as well.

One of my other goals was to publish a certain number of books per year. How was I going to do this? I had a full-time job as a business broker. I am also a Pastor for a local church. I have a wife and son. Friends. Then there is my own personal time. It was a dilemma. I knew I had to create a habit of spending a certain amount of time each day to devote to writing my books. The secret was to look at all my schedules. My work schedule and appointment times. My church obligations and times. When my wife and I spent time together. My son's needs. Time I hang out with my friends. Then I needed to deduct time for sleep, and the leftover time I could write.

Sounds extremely challenging, doesn't it? It was! The secret was to find the days and patterns where my work schedule had time slots available. The benefit of being self-employed is that I get to make my own schedule. It took some effort, but with my handy-dandy day planner, I scheduled my one, two, or three hours a day I could devote to writing. I also prioritized what I wanted to write by the length of the book, and how much preliminary work on the structure and idea I had already accomplished. I created a good habit every Friday of scheduling my time for the following week, so I knew exactly when my writing times were. I could adjust them on the fly if any of my other responsibilities changed. As I am writing this book (in my slotted time), this will be the fourth scheduled book I will publish so far this year. It's the beginning of April 2025 as I'm typing this.

Good habits can help you achieve the goals you have written down. Goals require three major components: time, money, and attention. Depending on the goal, whether it is a short-term or long-term goal, allocating these components becomes important to achieving what you desire. A few years ago, my wife wanted to try her hand at pottery (no pun intended). She found a class that was held downtown one evening each week. It wasn't cheap, so she needed to make sure she wanted to invest both financially and the two hours a week she would be there. She had a vision of learning the craft, which drove her intention to get her hands dirty. At the end of the journey, she was super happy that she had decided to learn the art. It was relaxing, she liked her teacher and met some others in the class. It was relaxing to design pieces and see them to completion. Now we have several little items around the house that she personally made, so the reward of her effort is visible in our lives.

Can you take time and think of small goals you have that maybe, because of bad habits, you have not been able to pursue? As far as time goes, we, as a modern society, have created bad habits around time. Recent research suggests that between social media viewing and streaming television binge-watching, these two distractions take up an average of over five hours a day of our time. Are you in the bad habit of having your eyes glued to a phone, tablet, or television for far too long every day?

What are some goals you have to achieve that, if you took half that time and spent it focused on pursuing a goal, you may accomplish them? Are you spending several hundred dollars a month on items that do not add any true value or long-lasting happiness to your life?

What is a place you wanted to visit or items you want to own that would fulfill a goal that you believe you can't afford? Sometimes we don't realize we have tiny bad habits that add up to a blockade preventing us from achieving a goal in our hearts.

Maybe you have a goal of being your own boss or owning your own company. What if you wrote down a real goal and a plan to achieve that dream? How much time would you spend researching how to start? How would you adjust your budget and get your credit score up to have or borrow the upfront money you need? Would it be worth it to go to school and get a degree or earn a certificate so you can start that business?

The truth is, we are in our lives where our habits have taken us. You have heard the saying You can take the poor hand someone was dealt and give it to another person who will turn it into a winning hand. The patterns and habits we created when we were young seldom change in our adult life unless absolutely necessary. Highly successful people will tell you the best way to start a positive habitual life is to first make your bed when you get up in the morning. The simplest of tasks. Why do most beds not get made? Bad habits. The habit of oversleeping. The habit of laziness. The habit of lying in bed too long, looking at social media.

Your homework for this chapter is to sit down with your daily notebook and write down all the habits you are consciously aware of in your life. The good, the bad, and the ugly. Then ask the person who knows you the most, spends the most time with you, to tell you the habits they see that you have, good and bad. Once you have this list, consider which ones need to stay and which ones need to go. Ponder what your life could be like if you could create more positive habits that could help you achieve the goals you have written down for yourself this year.

Find a healthy place where you are utilizing your time, talent, and treasure to create good habits that result in you writing your goals down and achieving them at a steady pace. When you begin to center your good habits around achieving your goals and begin recognizing bad habits that prevent you from achieving them, your satisfaction meter will begin to rise. You will fill your life with more joy, a sense of accomplishment, and hope. These three pillars will help you build a life that will be an inspiration to others. Let's continue to grow!

Chapter 4 Achieve Your Goals Naturally

You always have the option to take shortcuts in life, and in some cases, it is a good thing. When it comes to writing down and achieving your goals, whenever possible, achieve your goals naturally. It is almost better if you don't achieve your goal than to achieve it in a manipulative way. Many times, when you take a shortcut or cheat to achieve your goal, you deny yourself the proper resistance to build the real muscle it takes to achieve something. As we discussed earlier on how important habits are in achieving your goal, bad habits will hinder that achievement. Taking shortcuts or cheating creates a bad habit.

Let's take the number one goal people cheat at, which is dieting or losing weight. Most of us at one point in our lives have made a goal to lose weight. The natural way to do that is to have a caloric deficit each day, remove processed sugar from your diet, and exercise on a regular basis. What is a caloric deficit? It means if you naturally burn 2000 calories a day through your normal life, work, and sleep, then you need to take in fewer than 2000 calories to have a deficit. To gain weight or muscle, you do the opposite. The best way I have found to have a deficit is to limit yourself, if you can medically, to one good meal a day, or three to four small snacks. Removing processed sugar from your diet will help. Find an exercise you enjoy and do it for at least thirty minutes a day.

How do most people cheat to achieve this goal? Diet pills and pharmaceutical drugs. I have seen this getting more prominent in the last several years, with everyone through social media being more body conscious. It works great since most people see immediate results. What the chemicals are doing in your body is quickly removing the easy fat. Unfortunately, it allows the individual to not make the needed sacrifices in their diet and exercise to sustain any true long-term weight loss. For most people, the pills or drugs slowly become less effective, or they hit a plateau and stop losing weight. This leads to depression, which leads to stress and stress eating, which puts the weight back on within the next few weeks or months, and the vicious cycle continues.

As a writer, I have seen the evil of Artificial Intelligence become a massive shortcut for authors wanting to have more books but not wanting to put in the time and effort to write something from their heart and soul. There is great temptation now in most areas of our lives, and with technology making things easier, we have become a more stagnant and lazier people. Hard work is a good thing. It builds character. Patience is a virtue. Patience creates strong perseverance. Yes, getting immediate results is fun, but it will be detrimental to you when the next time nothing goes your way.

I'm always reminded of singers or bands whose debut album goes platinum and record sales are through the roof. It seems they can do no wrong. When the time comes to produce a second record, the pressure and expectation can be overwhelming to achieve the same success. Many times, achieving immediate success can ruin the longevity of an artist. We used to call these "one hit wonders." When you take a shortcut in achieving an important goal, it could have the same effect and disable you in future achievements.

One of the biggest shortcuts we see in modern life is the use of credit cards to buy things you can't afford. That immediate gratification is needed in today's world. Half of the country is in credit card debt. In 2024, Americans recorded over one trillion in credit card debt that rolled over to 2025. We are not like our parents and grandparents, who saved money and bought things they could afford. We now live in a different world where marketing is the number one function of most companies. We are bombarded twenty-four hours a day. Advertisements, Pop-ups, spam emails, spam texts, and everywhere you go, someone is pushing something on you.

Achieving goals naturally becomes a huge challenge in today's world. You need to understand, though, that when you achieve a goal naturally, you are accomplishing two things. One, the goal for which you were hoping. Two, the skills, character, confidence, and trust in yourself that you needed. There was a study several years ago from a military trainer regarding men in their forties, fifties, and sixties who had developed the cursed man boobs syndrome. The study took a hundred of those men and set them on a goal to achieve the natural ability to do fifty pushups at one time. The 100 men who started the study had an average of only sixteen pushups at one time. They put them on a daily exercise routine for ten weeks.

Each day in the first week, they were required to do thirty pushups with three sets of ten pushups. The next week, forty-five push-ups with three sets of fifteen.

Week three was sixty push-ups with three sets of twenty.
It continued with 75 with 3x25, 90 with 3x30, 105 with
3x35, 120 with 3x40, 135 with 3x45, and finally 150 with
3x50. For ten weeks, the 100 men attempted this routine.
By the end of the ten weeks, all the men had seen a
decrease in the fat around their chest, and they had
developed more strength in their chest, arms, shoulders,
and back. All of them said they felt more confident. They
all wanted to apply the same routine to other parts of
their body.

When you set out to achieve any goal, there will be
a sacrifice of time, money, character and self-identity.
Choosing your goals is crucial and should not be taken
lightly. Having small, medium and large goals to balance
all the sacrifices out is important too. If you have never
set goals before, always start with small achievable goals.
Don't begin goal setting with a large, time consuming,

impossible goal. That will ruin your goal setting life. Start with things that are within the achievable frame of your time, finances and confidence.

One of the ways I coach business owners to grow their business, and their network is to set time in their schedule to have weekly and monthly personal meetings with friends, clients, partners or employees. Quality time is the best currency in building your life or business. I have a minimum

of three or four meetings a month with my group of friends. A coffee, or lunch during the week. I also try to have a monthly gathering with a group of friends. A few years ago, I began doing things like karaoke nights, guys movie day, or wrestling nights watching WWE. Something that would be enjoyable and we could spend quality time breaking bread together and having fun. It was a small achievable goal which has had great reward in building strong friendships.

The reason I emphasize achieving your goals naturally is because when you cheat or use shortcuts it can lead to a false sense of achievement. The next goal you may not be able to cheat or take a short cut, and you will feel discouraged and start creating a low self-identity. Failure is okay. As long as you set a goal, do all you can to achieve it and fall short, the pursuit itself builds the tools you need for next time.

I think about the times I had to look for work. Did it suck having to send out all the resumes, fill out stupid tests, do zoom interviews with low level recruiters and still get turned down? Yes, it did. I have failed more interviews than I have won. Been turned down way more than chosen. The wisdom I gained through all the attempts, answering the questions, presenting myself in the best light, eventually put me in front of the right person and the right company. My good friend Michael Rubin always emphasizes the power of 'the first step!'

Setting goals is the 'first step!' Achieving them naturally is also a 'first step!' Sometimes we have to take a leap of faith. Sometimes we need to jump and pray the parachute opens. Sometimes we have to take our chips off the table, fold our cards and wait for the next hand. Achieving goals naturally takes time and is not always fun. The tools you earn by achieving naturally remain in your toolbox. You will find the more goals you achieve, the more tools you obtain, and the more dynamic your toolbox becomes. The more tools you acquire and the more confidence you build, the larger your goals can become.

Your homework for this chapter is to take some of the short-term goals you created in the second chapter and achieve them naturally. Once you have done that, make a note of the time it took. Notate what it costs you financially. Notate what habit, good or bad (hopefully good), helped you achieve that goal. Finally, what tool did you acquire by achieving that goal? Confidence? Growth? Wisdom? Hope? Write down what you gained, even if it was something physical, spiritual, emotional, financial, or relational. Now find a way to repeat that process on a slightly bigger goal. Let's keep growing!

Chapter 5 Celebrate Achieving Your Goals

The best part of achieving a goal is rewarding yourself for the accomplishment. Celebrate achieving your goals! Presenting yourself with a trophy of success, whatever that looks like. A day off, a nice dinner, new clothes, or a real trophy that says you did it. I know it is part of my process to register my books with the U.S. Copyright Office, but when I do get that letter in the mail with the Copyright Certificate, I treat that as a little reward for myself. I put it in a frame and hang it up, like a little diploma. Rewarding yourself is crucial to your own confidence, especially when you are writing down and achieving goals. You will miss several goals, so rewarding yourself for the ones you make helps ease the blow of the misses.

Even if they are small rewards, they can make a huge difference in your mental state moving forward. A reward makes you feel cared for. Like getting flowers, a card, or a nice email from a friend. For that moment, you feel special, so why not do that for yourself? A reward also creates contentment with your progress. Even if it was a small goal that didn't take you long to achieve, be content with the fact that you completed it, and let your heart feel content. Rewards are also good because they set markers between goals. Reward yourself with a little break before you start on the next one. If you had a little resentment about achieving that goal, the reward will help reduce that resentment. It may instill a stronger willpower to achieve the next goal. A reward can also re-energize you in case the last goal took a lot out of you.

A reward is great in increasing a positive state of mental health. Rewards release dopamine, which is crucial for all mankind to survive and live in peace with each other. Amazingly, you begin to train your brain that hard work pays off as you continue to write down your goals, achieve them, and reward yourself. You begin to find that the benefits begin to outweigh the costs. The harder your goals become, the better your rewards should be. This produces a subconscious determination as you expand your goals from small to medium and to large long-term goals.

Benefits begin to naturally occur, simple things like you develop less procrastination. Your mind gets used to working toward that goal and being rewarded, so when the next task comes, you get excited to begin, finish, and get another reward. You become more focused on the next goal. Your goals become deliberate in achieving an overall better life for you and your family. You create a system of good habits that generate positive reinforcement, which produces more accomplishments in your life.

What are some simple rewards you can start with after you finish achieving a goal and want to celebrate? Food rewards are always delicious. Splurge on some chocolate or ice cream, maybe a nice juicy steak, and a glass of wine or whiskey. Maybe you go out to eat or order in and binge-watch a show you've been wanting to see. I'm a movie buff, so I usually treat my wife, son and myself to a good movie, popcorn and coke. Maybe you are more into art and museums. Go take a day or afternoon and see a local show or exhibit. Take a day off!

Is there a special class you have been wanting to take? Pottery or yoga? Maybe you want to join a league, bowling, darts, axe throwing? My wife and I like to go to concerts, so many times a year we reward ourselves with live music. If you have the time and money, go away for the weekend. Take a Friday or Monday off and get out of town. It can be as simple as going to a coffee shop, having a nice latte and writing down your next goals. It can be big or small, but it needs to happen.

Celebrating the goals you have achieved is just as important as writing them down, creating good habits and achieving the goals themselves. If you really want to produce good emotions and opportunities in your life, keep track of your friends and family members' goals. When they achieve something, send them a small reward for their accomplishment.

Your homework for this chapter is to go back to the goals you set in chapter two regarding your spiritual life, physical life, emotional life, financial life, and relationships, and now attach a reward to each of those goals. Determine with what and how you wish to celebrate achieving each goal. If you can have them apply to the goal itself. Let's continue to grow!

Chapter 6 Keep Repeating and Expanding Your Goals

Some say, if at first you don't succeed, try and try again. In this case, for this chapter, I will say, when you succeed, succeed and succeed again. You will find that as you make small goals and achieve them, your brain will desire to do that exercise again. If you set a goal to read one book a month, maybe you will read two books a month. If you set a goal to lose five pounds and lose six, maybe you set another goal to lose 10 pounds. The secret is to capitalize on your successes. As a writer, I usually set myself a weekly goal of writing. Some weeks, I hit the goal before the week is over. It is tempting to stop since I reached the goal, but when I write another chapter or maybe two more, I feel great. It also gets me closer to finishing and publishing.

> Once you establish a good habit of creating, writing, setting your goals down, and completing them, the best thing to do is repeat the process and up the game a little bit. It is like weightlifting. Start with arm curls of fifteen pounds and do those consistently until they become too easy, then move to twenty pounds and start the process over. If you look at athletes, this is how they become professionals. They set goals, achieve them consistently, then raise the goal. A key secret to

becoming a goal setter and achiever is consistency. Find goals that are achievable and profitable for your well-being. Don't set your first goal to be an Oscar-winning actor. Set your first goal to take an acting class or become an extra on a movie set.

When I was living in Orlando. In the early 90's I took a job at the recently built Universal Studios Theme Park. Along with the theme park, they had ten working sound stages on the back lots. I knew I wanted to be in film and television, but I had no agent and no experience. I met one of the producers at the commissary one day and asked him what my first step should be. He advised me to get a headshot and take it to the extras office at the front of the back lots. It took me thirty days to get the photos done, but once I did, I walked them into the office and handed them to the front desk.

They took me down the hall, stood me against the wall, and took a Polaroid of my face (not sure why I needed the headshot). They said thank you and that they would call me.

The next morning, I got a call to be an extra on a television show they were shooting. It was a two-day shoot, and I got paid $75 a day, which in 1990 was pretty amazing. I loved every minute on the set; I smiled all the time and helped out wherever I could. Those two days were the most exciting I had had in a long time. I received my $150 that Friday at the office and wanted more.

A week later, one of the producers on the television show called me and said how impressed he was with my attitude and approach while on the set. He asked if I wanted to be (what was called back then) an extra regular. The show had an office scene as one of the regularly occurring scenes in the show. The producer wanted me to be a background office worker and appear in those scenes on a continual basis. It was a great opportunity, and my experience truly began in the film and television world.

Because I had a simple goal to start with, I achieved that goal by doing it to the best of my ability, the next level was presented, and I challenged myself to do more. It is one thing to set goals and achieve them; it is another to grow and continue that pattern, achieving a higher and higher level. If you can do this, it will bring great structure to your life, and you will create a pattern that will propel you to successful and amazing heights. If you remember the Harvard study, eighty-four percent of students never had goals.

I guarantee you that if ten successful people were lined up, they would all profess that goal setting was a crucial part of their journey. Most people who make excuses for their lack usually don't have a plan, have never written down their goals, and just wing it in life. Life consists of patterns, good and bad. As you begin to understand the importance of creating a pattern in your life of goal setting and achieving, you will see a huge difference between where you are going and where others do not practice this.

The WHACK life you can create is so important to you growing into a successful and consistent member of society. First, we write the goals down. Small, medium, and large goals. From there, we develop good habits to help work on and complete those goals. By creating good habits, you will achieve those goals naturally and feel the true reward of accomplishment. As you achieve each goal, make sure you celebrate that achievement, no matter how small it was, and reward yourself for the accomplishment. This changes the structure of your brain and creates a desire to set more goals. To be consistent and grow continually, the next phase is to keep repeating the pattern of goal setting and achieving. This will propel you into being a purposeful individual.

As you write down goals, achieve them, and repeat the process, slowly increase your benchmarks and expand your abilities. You have seen the before-and-after pictures of bodybuilders or people losing weight. Their growth is a result of the WHACK life. Be patient with your results. Don't quit if you fall short a few times. Learn from what went right and what went wrong. Keep a life journal of all your successes and failures. Calendar your progress and time-sensitive goals.

The last step in the WHACK life is the infamous and elusive 'Big, Hairy, Bodacious Goal'! These are long-term, giant goals you may have that are not for the faint of heart. These are usually things like buying a house, owning your own company, traveling the world, becoming a best-selling novelist, etc. These are usually achieved after years of perfecting small, medium, and large goals. Can they be achieved before that? Yes! Most of the time, you stumble into them, or chance and luck play a big part. It is important that each of us has a big, hairy, bodacious goal. One of my BHBGs is to self-finance and produce a feature film. Another one is to sell my *AREA FRH41* book series to Hulu, Netflix, or Amazon to be made into a series.

It is a giant task. It may never come to pass, but I wake up every day working towards the possibility. It is good to have something much bigger than you. Something that will ultimately require a little divine intervention for you to achieve. While you are perfecting your WHACK life with small, medium, and large goals, keep a few BHBGs in your back pocket. Who knows, stranger things have happened in life! Visit a bookstore and find a few biographies of famous people, and I assure you, they had some BHBGs, and some of them came true.

One more area to cover in our WHACK life. I hope you are getting excited about the future. Let's continue to grow!

Chapter 7 Become Infectious

My prayer in all this is that whoever reads this book walks away with the desire to become a better goal setter. I know personally my life has been far more productive and rewarding since I became goal-oriented. I continue to write down new goals, set time frames, and work to achieve them naturally. I do reward myself for achieving even the simplest of goals. Now the final phase of your WHACK life is to pay it forward. Become infectious. Your final homework is for you to write down at least five individuals in your life, family, friend, or co-worker who could use this knowledge.

Maybe you have overheard conversations like this: "I wish I could do this!" Or "I wish I could go there!" Maybe you have heard this statement, "I wish I had time to do this!" All these are red flags of someone who has not taken the time to sit down and write their goals and dreams down. Someone who believes it is not worth the effort. Unfortunately, like the Harvard study showed, it is, on average 80% of the people you may know. For many years, and as many books that come out regarding goal setting, I am still surprised how many people still don't make the effort to see if it really helps.

Your testimony could mean everything. Discussing with others how you started small and achieved a few little goals in your life. How you started challenging yourself to do more, go bigger, and dream crazier. I find that anytime I am doing a one-on-one with someone new from a networking group, at some time during the conversation, I ask them what the goals were that they wrote down at the beginning of the year. At that point, I usually receive a strange stare from them, as if this is the first time someone has asked them that question. They usually respond with, "Do you mean my New Year's resolution?"

At this point, I spend the next ten minutes explaining the difference between a goal and a resolution. I also provide a quick testimony of all the cool things I have done and accomplished by being goal-oriented. I try to become infectious. In the hopes that they will get even a tiny spark to attempt having a WHACK life. At that point, I help them write three simple goals they can accomplish that month.

In a crazy world where most people are out to get each other, or convince us falsely that we are divided, I try to show how we all are on the same journey in this life, and helping each other achieve even the smallest of things brings hope and faith back into our lives. So, your last homework assignment is to become infectious by sharing the joy of becoming goal-oriented. I hope this book has blessed you and given you a few nuggets to make your life more purposeful and productive.

I will recommend a follow-up to *The WHACK life*, another book that goes along with this book, entitled *The 100 Things I Will Do This Year!* This book is a journal designed to help you write down one hundred small goals you want to accomplish in a calendar year. These two books will be great tools for you to become a more determined, accomplished, and fulfilled individual. Who knows, maybe in a year or so you will write down that

Big Hairy Bodacious Goal and make it happen! May God bless your efforts and grant you the vision and wisdom to set the right goals that will give you the courage and desire to have an amazing life. I look forward to hearing your testimonies. Happy Goal Setting! Happy Goal Achieving! Happy Goal Celebrating! Have a wonderful journey

Please enjoy these other books from Todd Hutchinson:

The Puzzle of You and I
Learning to solve life's puzzles

AREA FRH41: Book 1 Happy Howloween

AREA FRH41: Book 2 Curse of Roanoke
AREA FRH41: Book 3 Ghoul of Garrison Mine

Supernatural Fiction Series

10 Films

A Journey to Produce 10 Films

6 to 7

ghostwritten for Michael D. Rubin.

A journey from a six-figure

to a seven-figure annual income

All titles are available on Amazon.com or at

www.tksbooks.com.

Happy Reading!

www.ingramcontent.com/pod-product-compliance
Lightning Source LLC
LaVergne TN
LVHW051428080426
835508LV00022B/3301